Sausages

Rachel Green

Making the most of the Great British Sausage

Photography by Michael Powell

First published in Great Britain in 2009
by Green Shoots, Beech House, Kingerby, Market Rasen
Lincolnshire LN8 3PF
Green Shoots is a trading name of
Green Shoots Enterprise Ltd
Text copyright © Rachel Green 2009
Design © Green Shoots 2009

Designer Debbie Lishman
Photography © Michael Powell 2009 www.michaelpowell.com

Recipe reproduction
with kind permission of
www.peas.org
www.britishcarrots.co.uk
www.scholes-ltd.co.uk

A CIP record for this book is available from the
British Library
Printed by GSB, Lincolnshire
ISBN 978-0-9556216-1-1

Sausages

Foreword

by Jimmy Doherty

You won't be surprised to hear that I value the meat of the pig above that of all other animals! No other animal is so versatile in its eating. And from all that the pig has to offer, the sausage gives the cook a wealth of choice.

At home, at breakfast, lunch or dinner, for children's tea or on the barbie, on a picnic, in a lunchbox or at a wedding, we Brits enjoy our sausages on every conceivable occasion.

Of course no two sausages are the same, and in my opinion, provenance is vital.

Make the effort to search out sausages from a happy, well fed, truly free-range pig (and I'm sure you know where to find them...) and you will gain even more pleasure from Rachel's delicious and inspiring collection of recipes.

Happy cooking, and happy eating!

Jimmy

Rachel Green

Who doesn't love sausages? It is rare to meet anyone, from nine to ninety who doesn't enjoy a really good quality British sausage. I have found myself cooking different versions of the sausage all over the country and in a great variety of ways. Of course as a Lincolnshire lass, I love the Lincolnshire sausage with its delicious sage and pepper, but a Cumberland sausage or a Suffolk sausage is a very fine thing too.

I do hope you enjoy this celebration of sausages in all their glory. They are the perfect convenience food, and can be whipped into something delicious and different for every occasion. I know I am not alone amongst chefs in loving sausages and have been inspired by many. I would like to thank Jimmy for his words and ongoing support of British pig farmers.

I must thank all sorts of wonderful people who have helped to bring together this cornucopia of sausages – Sue Richmond, for all her support and attention to detail, Jeni Barrett for her eagle eyes, Kathleen, Marija, Alison and Charlotte too. Also Stephen Hallam for his encouragement and Gill Pawson who inspired me to get on with it and write the book. My dear friend Gee and of course my son Ollie who is my most honest critic!

And I am proud to support Help for Heroes, a wonderful non-political charity helping our wounded from Iraq and Afghanistan.

Sausages were called bangers during the Second World War because they contained so much water they exploded when fried

Sausages

for breakfast
and brunch

Sausage, Bacon and Potato Frittata

2 tbsp rapeseed oil
30g butter
3 potatoes, peeled and diced
1 onion, peeled and finely sliced
4 good quality pork sausages,
cooked and cut into 2cm slices
4 rashers streaky bacon, sliced
8 eggs
200ml double cream
Nutmeg, freshly grated
2 small red peppers,
deseeded and diced
100g Cheddar cheese, grated
2 tbsp parsley, finely chopped
Sea salt and black pepper

Serves 6 – 8

Heat the rapeseed oil and butter in a large, non-stick frying pan. Add the diced potato and cook over a gentle heat for 5 minutes, without browning. Add the onion and cook for 10 minutes, stirring regularly, until the potatoes are nearly tender. Add the sausages and bacon, increase the heat slightly, and cook for a further 5 minutes.

Meanwhile, whisk the eggs with the cream and season well with sea salt, pepper and freshly grated nutmeg. Stir in the peppers, cheese and the parsley. Pour this mixture over the sausage, bacon and potatoes in the pan, and cook very slowly, moving the contents of the pan around gently until the frittata begins to set. Keep loosening the mixture around the edges and shake the pan so that the bottom of the frittata does not stick.

When the frittata is just firm, invert it onto a large plate and then slide it back into the pan the other way up. Cook on this side for 5 minutes and then slide onto a clean serving plate or board. To serve, cut into wedges.

Country Sausage and Potato Hash

Preheat the grill to high. Quarter the red pepper and grill, skin side up, until the skins are charred. Transfer to a bowl, cover with cling film and leave to cool. Turn the grill down to medium and grill the sausages; this should take 10 – 15 minutes. Turn regularly to ensure they brown evenly. When cool, peel the red peppers and cut into strips.

Place the potatoes in a large pan of salted water and bring to the boil. Simmer until just tender, drain well and set aside.

Melt the butter with the rapeseed oil in a large frying pan. Fry the onion for 5 minutes, then add the potatoes and fry for a further 5 minutes, until the potatoes are starting to brown. Add the red peppers and paprika, reduce the heat and cook gently for 10 minutes, turning the mixture occasionally without breaking it up too much.

Add the tomatoes, spring onions and parsley and season well with sea salt and black pepper. Cook for a further minute until all is piping hot. Sprinkle the cheese over the top and place under the grill for 3 – 4 minutes until golden brown. Serve on a warm plate and top with the sausages.

1 red pepper
8 good quality pork sausages
4 potatoes,
peeled and cut into 3cm cubes
55g butter
1 tbsp rapeseed oil
1 onion,
peeled and finely chopped
½ tsp paprika
2 tomatoes,
skinned and roughly chopped
4 spring onions,
trimmed and finely sliced
2 tbsp parsley, finely chopped
30g mature Cheddar cheese,
grated
Sea salt and black pepper

Serves 4

Preheat the grill to high

Mediterranean Sausages with Rocket and Fig Salad

Heat the rapeseed oil in a frying pan over a medium heat and brown the sausages on all sides for 5 minutes. Add the garlic, chopped tomatoes and parsley, reduce the heat and cook for a further 5 minutes. Season to taste with sea salt and freshly ground black pepper. Keep warm until ready to use.

Meanwhile, cut the figs in half lengthways. Mix the balsamic vinegar, brown sugar and cinnamon together in a bowl, add the figs and gently toss to coat. Leave to marinate whilst you heat the grill. When ready, grill the figs for 5 minutes per side, reserving any juices in the bowl. Do not overcook or the figs will become mushy.

To make the dressing, whisk together the reserved marinade with the rapeseed oil, lemon juice and Dijon mustard and season to taste.

Place the rocket and the cooled figs in a large salad bowl, toss with the dressing and serve with the sausages.

4 good quality pork sausages
2 tbsp rapeseed oil
2 cloves garlic,
peeled and crushed
2 large tomatoes,
roughly chopped
2 tbsp parsley, finely chopped
Sea salt and black pepper

For the rocket and fig salad
4 large figs
2 tbsp balsamic vinegar
2 tsp dark brown sugar
Pinch ground cinnamon
3 tbsp rapeseed oil
3 tsp freshly squeezed
lemon juice
1 tsp Dijon mustard
110g rocket leaves

Serves 4

The Perfect Sausage Sandwich

1 large baguette, cut into 4
8 pork sausages
2 large onions, sliced
1 tbsp rapeseed oil
2 tbsp runny honey

Serves 4

Heat the rapeseed oil in a frying pan and slowly cook the sausages for about 10 – 15 minutes until golden brown and cooked through. Remove and keep warm. Add the onions to the pan and cook over a low heat until soft, about 15 minutes. Increase the heat, stir in the honey and allow the onions to caramelise.

Meanwhile, split the baguette slices in half horizontally and lightly toast the cut sides. Pile the sausages into the baguette along with the onions, cut in half and serve with the ketchup and mustard relish alongside in a small pot.

Tomato and Mustard Relish

5 tbsp tomato ketchup
3 tsp English mustard

Mix the ketchup and mustard together and season with sea salt and black pepper. Serve with sausages.

Sausages Wrapped in Bacon with Sweetcorn Fritters and Honey

Using the back of a knife, stretch each bacon rasher out – this will stop them shrinking as they cook. Wrap a rasher of bacon around each sausage and place on a non-stick baking sheet. Cook under the preheated grill, turning occasionally until sausages are browned, approximately 10 minutes.

Meanwhile make the sweetcorn fritters. Sift the flour into a large mixing bowl and make a well in the centre. Whisk the egg yolks and milk together with the parsley, chives and paprika and gradually add to the flour, whisking until smooth. Stir in the sweetcorn and spring onions and season with sea salt and plenty of black pepper. In a clean bowl whisk the egg whites until they form soft peaks and fold into the batter using a metal spoon. Heat the rapeseed oil in a frying pan and ladle spoonfuls of the batter into the pan to make individual fritters in batches of 3. This mixture should make 12 fritters. Fry the fritters for 2 – 3 minutes on each side or until golden brown.

Drizzle the fritters with the runny honey and serve with the bacon wrapped sausages.

8 rashers smoked streaky bacon
8 good quality pork sausages

For the fritters
110g self-raising flour
2 eggs, separated
125ml milk
1 tbsp parsley, finely chopped
1 tbsp chives, finely chopped
Pinch paprika
170g sweetcorn kernels,
drained and rinsed
4 spring onions,
trimmed and finely chopped
1 tbsp rapeseed oil
2 tbsp runny honey
Sea salt and black pepper

Serves 4

Preheat the grill to high

Sausage Eggs Benedict

First make the hollandaise sauce. Place the egg yolks and lemon juice in a fairly large bowl and season. Whisk all the ingredients until they have blended together. Place over a pan of just simmering water, making sure that the bowl is not in contact with the water. Whisk in the butter, a few cubes at a time, until the sauce begins to thicken. Continue adding the butter, whisking all the time and adding a splash of water if the hollandaise looks like it is becoming too thick. If the sauce begins to separate, remove from the heat immediately and add a teaspoon of cold water to the mixture.

Once all of the butter has been incorporated season to taste with sea salt and black pepper, if required and lemon juice. Remove from the heat and keep the hollandaise warm.

Next, prepare the eggs and sausages. Preheat the grill to a moderate heat and grill the sausages for 10 – 15 minutes. At the same time, poach the eggs in a large saucepan of barely simmering water to which you have added the white wine vinegar. You will have to do this in two batches. When the eggs and sausages are almost ready, cut the muffins in half and place them in the toaster or under the grill. When the muffins have been lightly toasted, butter them generously and place in the middle of a warmed plate.

Remove the sausages from the grill and place on top of each half muffin. Place a poached egg on top of the sausage and finally spoon the warmed hollandaise sauce over the egg. Sprinkle with cayenne pepper and serve immediately.

8 good quality pork sausages
8 eggs
1 tsp white wine vinegar
4 English muffins
Softened butter

For the hollandaise sauce
4 egg yolks
2 tbsp lemon juice
250g unsalted butter,
cut into small dice and chilled
Cayenne pepper
Sea salt & black pepper (optional)

Serves 4

Preheat the grill

Sausages

Sage Pancakes with Sausage, Red Onion and Mustard

For the pancakes
110g plain flour
1 egg, lightly beaten
290ml milk
1 tbsp sage, finely chopped
Rapeseed oil, for frying

For the filling
8 good quality pork sausages
1 tbsp rapeseed oil
2 red onions,
peeled and finely sliced
1 tsp brown sugar
2 large tomatoes,
skinned and chopped
Dijon mustard, to serve
Sea salt and black pepper

Makes 8

Preheat the grill

Sift the flour into a bowl, season with sea salt and black pepper and make a well in the centre. Pour in the egg and 50ml of milk and whisk, gradually drawing the flour in from the sides. Keep mixing and adding a little more milk until all the flour has been incorporated and you have a smooth batter which should be the consistency of single cream. Stir in the sage, then cover the mixture and set aside in the refrigerator for 30 minutes.

Meanwhile grill the sausages for 10 – 15 minutes, turning regularly, until golden brown and cooked through. Whilst the sausages are cooking, heat the tablespoon of rapeseed oil in a pan, add the onions and brown sugar and fry gently for 10 – 15 minutes until soft and slightly caramelised. Thickly slice the sausages.

To cook the pancakes, heat a little rapeseed oil in a frying pan over a medium heat. Pour in enough batter to cover the base of the pan and swirl around quickly. Cook for 1 – 2 minutes until the bottom side is golden brown. Use a fish slice to flip the pancake and cook for a further minute. Transfer to a warm plate and keep warm whilst cooking the rest of the pancakes.

To serve, spread each pancake with a little Dijon mustard. Add the sliced sausages, caramelised onions and chopped tomatoes. Fold each pancake into quarters and serve with a green salad.

Pancakes can be quite fiddly and time-consuming to cook, but they can be prepared beforehand. Simply layer them on a warm plate with a small piece of greaseproof paper in between each one, then cover the plate with foil and keep warm until required.

Sausage and Scrambled Egg Burritos

First prepare the tomato salsa. Combine the tomatoes, garlic and chilli in the bowl of a food processor and roughly chop. Add the vinegar and sugar and season well. Pulse to combine the mixture, stir in the coriander and place in a small bowl and set aside until ready to serve.

Heat 1 tablespoon of the rapeseed oil in a large pan over a medium heat and brown the sausages on all sides, this will take 10 – 15 minutes. Remove the sausages from the pan, cool slightly and cut into thin slices and keep warm.

Heat the remaining oil in the pan. Add the onion and green pepper to the pan and cook over a medium heat, stirring occasionally for 5 – 10 minutes, until they have started to soften. Add the beaten eggs to the pan and scramble over a medium heat, stirring constantly, until the eggs are almost set. Remove from the heat and stir in the sliced sausages.

Fill each tortilla with the sausage and egg mixture, roll up and place, seam side down, on a lightly greased baking sheet, sprinkle with cheese and place in the preheated oven for 5 minutes. Slice each burrito in half and serve hot with the salsa on the side.

4 good quality pork sausages
2 tbsp rapeseed oil
1 onion,
peeled and finely chopped
1 green pepper,
deseeded and chopped
8 eggs, beaten
8 flour tortillas
110g Cheddar cheese, grated
Sea salt and black pepper

For the salsa
110g cherry tomatoes, quartered
1 clove garlic,
peeled and crushed
1 green chilli,
deseeded and finely chopped
1 tbsp red wine vinegar
Pinch of caster sugar
1 tbsp fresh coriander, chopped

Serves 4

Preheat oven to
200°C/400°F/Gas Mark 6

Sausages

Mexican Ranch-Style Eggs with Chorizo Sausage

Heat 2 tablespoons of the oil in a frying pan, add the onion and garlic and sauté for 5 minutes until just softened. Add the tomatoes and chorizo and cook for a further 2 minutes, then add the chilli and cook for another 3 – 4 minutes. Season with sea salt and black pepper and keep warm.

Heat the remaining oil in a frying pan and fry the eggs in batches until the whites are set and the yolks are creamy. Divide the tomato and chorizo mixture onto 4 plates and top with eggs, serve with warm flour tortillas.

4 tbsp rapeseed oil
1 onion,
peeled and finely chopped
2 cloves garlic,
peeled and finely chopped
280g ripe tomatoes, chopped
225g chorizo sausage,
thickly sliced
1 green chilli,
deseeded and finely chopped
Sea salt and black pepper
8 eggs
4 flour tortillas, warmed, to serve

Serves 4

There are more than 470 recipes and flavours for sausages in Britain. If you take into account all the different variations from butchers across the country, you could eat a different British sausage every day for ten years.

Sausages

for Lunch

Pan-fried Sausages with Peppers and Basil

2 orange peppers
2 yellow peppers
4 tbsp rapeseed oil
8 garlicky sausages
2 red onions,
peeled and cut into chunks
2 cloves garlic,
peeled and crushed
Handful fresh basil leaves
Sea salt and black pepper

Serves 4

Preheat the grill to high

Place the peppers on a baking sheet and grill, turning regularly, until the skin is black all over. Remove to a bowl, cover with clingfilm and leave to cool. Once the peppers are cool enough to handle, peel them, remove the seeds and cut each pepper into large strips. Place in a bowl with half the rapeseed oil and the garlic. Roughly tear the basil leaves and add to the peppers. Season well and set aside.

Heat the remaining rapeseed oil in a large frying pan and add the sausages and onions. Pan fry the sausages for around 10 – 15 minutes until they are golden brown all over and cooked through, and the onions are soft and caramelised. Add the peppers and stir well.

Serve with warm, crusty bread and a green salad.

Summer Sausage, Bacon and Egg Salad

Boil the eggs for 7 minutes, drain and run under cold water to stop them cooking. Leave to cool, then peel and cut into quarters. Pan fry the bacon rashers until golden brown and crisp, and drain on kitchen paper.

Heat half the rapeseed oil in a large frying pan, add the sausages and red peppers, and cook over a medium heat until browned and cooked through. Remove the sausages and peppers from the pan, add the remaining rapeseed oil, and fry the cubes of bread, turning regularly, for 2 – 3 minutes until they are golden brown all over.

To make the dressing, whisk all the ingredients together and season. To assemble the salad, arrange the salad leaves, chicory and green beans on a large serving platter or in a salad bowl. Add the sausages and peppers, croutons, bacon and finally the quarters of egg. Drizzle with the salad dressing and garnish with the chopped chives.

4 eggs
4 rashers streaky bacon
2 tbsp rapeseed oil
4 good quality pork sausages,
sliced
1 red pepper,
deseeded and diced
2 thick slices white bread,
cut into 2 cm cubes
Handful mixed salad leaves
1 head each,
red and white chicory
200g green beans,
topped, tailed and blanched
1 tbsp chives, finely chopped
Sea salt and black pepper

For the dressing
1 clove garlic,
peeled and crushed
3 tbsp rapeseed oil
2 tbsp lemon juice
1 tbsp balsamic vinegar
1 tsp Dijon mustard

Serves 4

Sausages

Sausage, Shallot and Borlotti Bean Soup

Heat the rapeseed oil in a heavy-based sauté pan or saucepan. Add the shallots and sausages and sauté for 5 – 10 minutes, browning them all over. Add the carrots and sauté for a further 3 minutes. Add the garlic and cook for 30 seconds, then add the tinned tomatoes, tomato purée, borlotti beans, wine, stock, sugar and bay leaf. Season well with sea salt and black pepper. Bring to the boil and simmer for 15 minutes on a low heat. If the soup becomes too thick, add a little more stock, and then add the shredded cabbage and the parsley. Mix well and cook for a further 5 minutes, until the cabbage is just cooked.

Remove the sausages and slice each one into three. Divide between warmed serving bowls and pour over all the bean soup. Garnish with a little more parsley and serve with warm bread.

2 tbsp rapeseed oil
12 shallots,
peeled and left whole
8 Toulouse or spicy sausages
1 carrot, peeled and finely diced
3 cloves garlic,
peeled and finely chopped
1 x 400g tin chopped
plum tomatoes
½ tbsp tomato purée
1 x 400g tin borlotti beans,
drained and rinsed
55ml red wine
700 ml chicken stock
1 bay leaf
1 tsp caster sugar
150g Savoy cabbage,
finely shredded
2 tbsp parsley, finely chopped,
plus extra to garnish
Sea salt and black pepper

Serves 4 – 6

Fast Sausage Cassoulet

1 tbsp rapeseed oil
8 good quality pork sausages
2 tbsp rapeseed oil
1 red onion, peeled and diced
2 cloves garlic,
peeled and crushed
8 mushrooms, cut into quarters
1 bay leaf
6 juniper berries, crushed
1 sprig thyme
200ml red wine
1 tbsp redcurrant jelly
1 tbsp tomato ketchup
½ tbsp balsamic vinegar
1 x 400g tin green lentils
1 x 400g tin haricot beans
Sea salt and black pepper

Serves 4

Heat the rapeseed oil in a frying pan and brown the sausages well on all sides. Set aside. Heat the rapeseed oil in a large casserole dish or saucepan and add the red onion. Cover and cook over a medium to low heat for 5 – 10 minutes, until softened. Remove the lid and add the garlic, cook for 1 minute, then add the mushrooms and cook for a further 5 minutes.

Add the bay leaf, juniper berries and thyme, then add the red wine, redcurrant jelly, tomato ketchup and balsamic vinegar. Bring to the boil, stir well and turn down to a simmer. Rinse the lentils and haricot beans and add to the pan, along with the sausages. Mix together well and adjust the seasoning as necessary. Simmer for 10 minutes, until the sausages are cooked through, and serve.

Griddled Sausages with Salsa Verde and Squash Gratin

To make the salsa verde, place the parsley, lemon zest, capers and garlic in a food processor and blitz until finely chopped. Add the lemon juice, rapeseed oil and mustard and season to taste with sea salt and black pepper. Set aside until ready to use.

Meanwhile prepare the squash gratin. Heat the rapeseed oil in a medium-sized saucepan, then add the onion, garlic and squash and cook gently until softened but not browned. Add the thyme and season with sea salt and black pepper.

Layer the squash mixture with the grated cheese in a buttered ovenproof dish. In a small pan, bring the cream and milk to the boil, season and pour over the squash. Bake for 30 – 40 minutes until the squash is tender and the top of the gratin is golden brown.

Heat a ridged griddle pan over a high heat and drizzle lightly with some rapeseed oil. Griddle the sausages on all sides until golden brown and cooked through. Garnish the squash gratin with some thyme leaves and serve with the sausages and salsa verde.

8 good quality pork sausages
Rapeseed oil

For the salsa verde
3 tbsp flat-leaf parsley
Juice and zest of 1 small lemon
2 tbsp capers,
drained and rinsed
2 cloves garlic,
peeled and crushed
150ml rapeseed oil
½ tbsp Dijon mustard

For the squash gratin
2 tbsp rapeseed oil
1 onion,
peeled and finely chopped
2 cloves garlic,
peeled and finely chopped
1kg butternut squash,
peeled, deseeded and
cut into 3cm cubes
2 – 3 thyme sprigs, leaves
picked, plus extra to garnish
150g Cheddar cheese,
finely grated
Softened butter, for greasing
290ml double cream
150ml full fat milk
Sea salt and black pepper

Serves 4 – 6

Preheat the oven to
190°C/375°F/Gas Mark 5

Toad in the Hole

Place the sausages in a large metal roasting tin, spaced apart. Drizzle with the rapeseed oil and bake for 10 – 15 minutes until the sausages are starting to colour.

To make the batter, sift the flour and mustard powder into a bowl, make a well in the centre, beat the eggs with the milk and half of the water, tip the mixture into the well and incorporate the flour into the liquid and beat until you have a smooth batter. Season the batter with sea salt and black pepper, place the bowl in the fridge for at least 30 minutes, the batter can be made in advance.

Remove the sausages from the oven and if they haven't released much fat, add another 1 – 2 tbsp of oil to the tray. Take the batter out of the fridge and add the remaining 55ml cold water, whisk well. Place the roasting tin on a direct heat and get the oil and the roasting tray very hot. Add the batter and place in the hot oven on the highest shelf and cook for a further 35 – 40 minutes, until the toad is fully risen and golden.

12 good quality pork sausages
2 tbsp rapeseed oil

For the batter
150g plain flour
Pinch English mustard powder
2 large eggs
150ml milk
110ml water
Sea salt and black pepper

Serves 4 – 6

Preheat the oven to
220°C/425°F/Gas Mark 7

This traditional dish is delicious served with onion gravy or cauliflower cheese, and makes a warming and filling winter lunch. (See Accompaniments)

As a variation, try wrapping the sausages in bacon.

Sausages

Sausage, Tomato and Basil Lasagne with Mozzarella

8 good quality pork sausages,
grilled and cut into slices
300g fresh lasagne sheets
2 x 150g balls of mozzarella,
torn into pieces
Parmesan cheese, for grating
2 tbsp rapeseed oil
Handful basil leaves, to garnish

For the tomato sauce
2 tbsp rapeseed oil
3 garlic cloves,
peeled and sliced
1 bay leaf
Handful of basil leaves, chopped
2 x 400g tins good quality
Italian plum tomatoes
Sea salt and black pepper

For the cheese sauce
30g butter
30g plain flour
570ml full fat milk
110g Parmesan cheese, grated
Pinch nutmeg

Serves 4 – 6

Preheat the oven to
180°C/350°F/Gas Mark 4

First make the tomato sauce. Heat the rapeseed oil in a saucepan and fry the garlic until just coloured. Add the bay leaf, basil and the tinned tomatoes, season with sea salt and black pepper and cook gently for 30 minutes with a lid on, stirring occasionally. Add the sliced sausages and cook for a further 5 minutes, then remove from the heat, discard the bay leaf and check the seasoning. If the sauce begins to look a little thick, add a splash of water. Set aside until ready to use.

Next make the cheese sauce. Melt the butter in a saucepan, stir in the flour and cook for 1 – 2 minutes. Take the pan off the heat and gradually whisk in the milk. Return to the heat and bring to the boil, stirring all the time. Simmer gently for 2 minutes until thickened and season with sea salt and black pepper. Remove from the heat and add the Parmesan and a pinch of nutmeg.

Grease an ovenproof baking dish. Place some of the tomato and sausage sauce in the bottom of the dish, top with some lasagne sheets and then the cheese sauce. Repeat the layers until you have filled the dish, finishing with a layer of the cheese sauce. Arrange the mozzarella on the top and grate some Parmesan cheese over. Drizzle with the rapeseed oil and bake in the preheated oven for 40 – 45 minutes until golden brown and bubbling. Garnish with basil leaves and serve.

Spring Onion and Potato Rösti with Sausage and Tomato Raclette

Cook the sausages either under the grill, in the oven or in a frying pan with a little rapeseed oil. Slice into 3cm rounds.

Boil the potatoes in their skins for 8 minutes, allow to cool and then peel. Coarsely grate the potatoes into a large bowl, stir in the spring onion, garlic and parsley and season with sea salt and black pepper.
Shape the mixture into 8 rösti, place on a tray and refrigerate to chill for 10 – 15 minutes.

Heat the rapeseed oil in a frying pan and fry the rösti for 4 minutes on each side until crisp and golden, drain on kitchen paper. Place the rösti on a baking sheet and top with the rounds of sausage, chopped tomatoes and sliced raclette cheese. Place under a preheated grill until melted and golden.

Serve with a tomato chutney. (see accompaniments)

8 good quality sausages
4 medium baking potatoes, scrubbed
1 bunch spring onions, finely sliced
1 clove garlic, peeled and crushed
2 tbsp parsley, finely chopped
6 tbsp rapeseed oil
2 tomatoes, roughly chopped
225g raclette cheese rounds
Sea salt and black pepper

Serves 4

Preheat oven to
200°C/400°F/Gas Mark 6

Preheat the grill to high

If you can't find raclette you could use Emmenthal, Gruyere or Jarlsberg for this Alpine-inspired dish.

Sausages

Sausage and Lentil Salad with Roasted Squash

Put the butternut squash into a bowl, add the garlic, chilli and rapeseed oil, season with sea salt and black pepper and mix well. Tip onto a baking tray and roast in the preheated oven for 25 – 30 minutes until softened and golden. Remove from the oven and set aside.

For the lentil salad, mix all the ingredients together in a mixing bowl and season with sea salt and black pepper.

Grill the sausages on a medium setting for 10 – 15 minutes, until lightly browned, cool slightly and cut into slices.

Divide the lentil salad between 4 plates and top with slices of hot sausage and roasted squash. Drizzle with rapeseed oil before serving.

For the roasted squash
1 butternut squash, peeled, deseeded and cut into chunks
2 garlic cloves, peeled and finely chopped
½ red chilli, deseeded and finely chopped
2 tbsp rapeseed oil, plus extra for drizzling
Sea salt and black pepper

For the lentil salad
2 tbsp rapeseed oil
1 tbsp balsamic vinegar
110g puy lentils, cooked
180g green beans, blanched, refreshed and chopped
1 tbsp parsley, finely chopped
1 tbsp chives, finely chopped
1 tbsp coriander, finely chopped
8 good quality pork sausages

Serves 4

Preheat the oven to
200°C/400°F/Gas Mark 6

Sausages

The word sausage
is derived from the
Latin word salsus
which means
something salted

Sausages

barbecue
and picnics

Barbecued Lincolnshire Sausages with Charred Tomato Salsa

8 Lincolnshire sausages
4 large tomatoes, halved
½ red chilli, finely chopped
1 red onion,
peeled and finely chopped
1 clove garlic,
peeled and finely chopped
A small handful fresh basil, torn
1 tbsp coriander leaves, chopped
½ tsp brown sugar
2 tbsp rapeseed oil
½ tbsp red wine vinegar
Sea salt and black pepper

To serve
4 small baguettes / crusty rolls
Soft butter (optional)
Rocket leaves, washed

Serves 4

Barbecue the sausages for 10 – 15 minutes, until cooked through. For the salsa, barbecue the tomato halves until the skins start to blacken. Transfer to a bowl and set aside until cool enough to handle.

Roughly chop the tomatoes, stir in the rest of the ingredients and season well. Warm the baguettes or crusty rolls, then split in half and butter if desired, spread with the salsa, add some rocket leaves and top with a couple of sausages.

This recipe can also be made using a griddle pan, heat the pan until smoking, brush with ½ tablespoon rapeseed oil and cook the sausages and tomatoes as above.

Pork and Stilton Sausage Rolls

Put the sausage meat into a large bowl, add the stilton, parsley and sage, season with sea salt and black pepper and mix well.

Roll out the pastry on a lightly-floured surface to form an oblong and cut into 2 strips. Divide the sausage mixture in half and shape each half into a long sausage. Lay this down the centre of each pastry strip. Brush the edges of the pastry with the beaten egg and fold over to seal. Crimp the sealed edges with a fork. Cut each strip into 6 pieces.

Divide the sausage rolls between 2 lightly-greased baking sheets, making sure they are well spaced apart. Make 2 snips in the pastry using scissors, this helps release the steam from the sausage meat and keeps the pastry crisp. Brush the tops with the remaining beaten egg and bake for 15 – 20 minutes, until golden brown.

450g pork sausage meat
150g Stilton, crumbled
2 tbsp parsley, finely chopped
1 tbsp sage, finely chopped
1 x 500g pack good
quality puff pastry
Plain flour, for rolling pastry
1 egg, lightly beaten
Sea salt and black pepper

Makes 12

Preheat the oven to
220°C/425°F/Gas Mark 7

Sausage rolls always make ideal picnic food, but with the addition of Stilton these also make perfect canapés for Christmas. Simply cut them a little smaller for the perfect festive mouthful!

Sausages

Grandma Jessie's Sausage and Apple Pie

Roll out half the pastry and use it to line a 23cm / 9 in pie plate. Mix the chopped sage into the sausage meat and season well with sea salt, black pepper and the ground nutmeg. Place half of the sausage meat over the pastry base, leaving a border around the edge. Cover with the thinly sliced apples, then top with the rest of the sausage meat mixture. Roll out the rest of the pastry. Brush the border of the bottom half of the pie with the beaten egg and cover with the remaining pastry, pressing down well to seal. Crimp the edges of the pie and cut a cross in the centre for the steam to escape whilst cooking. Place in the fridge for 30 minutes.

Brush the pie with the remaining beaten egg and cook in the preheated oven for 10 minutes, before turning the heat down to 180°C/350°F/Gas Mark 4 and cooking for a further 30 – 40 minutes, until puffed up and golden brown. Leave for 10 minutes before serving.

1 x 500g pack good quality puff pastry
3 tbsp sage leaves, finely chopped
450g sausage meat
Pinch ground nutmeg
2 large Cox's or similar sharp tasting apples, peeled, cored and thinly sliced
Beaten egg to glaze
Sea salt and black pepper

Serves 4 – 6

Preheat oven to
220°C/450°F/Gas Mark 7

Sausages

Spicy Chorizo, New Potato and Tomato Pasties

150g chorizo sausage, sliced
350g new potatoes, cooked and cut into small pieces
110g Cheddar cheese, grated
110g sun-dried tomatoes, roughly chopped
1 tbsp chives
1 tbsp basil
3 tbsp mayonnaise
2 tbsp double cream
2 sheets ready rolled puff pastry
1 egg, beaten
Sea salt and black pepper

Makes 12

Preheat the oven to
200°C/400°F/Gas Mark 6

First prepare the filling. Place the chorizo, new potatoes, cheese, sun-dried tomatoes, chives, basil, mayonnaise and cream in a bowl, season with sea salt and black pepper, remembering that the chorizo and sun-dried tomatoes may be salty, and mix well.

Place the puff pastry sheets on a lightly floured surface and cut out 16 – 18 cm rounds, using a suitably sized saucer or bowl as a template. Place a spoonful of the filling in the middle of each pastry circle. Brush the edges with beaten egg, bring the edges together into a half moon shape and crimp to seal. Repeat with the remaining pasties. Place on a greased baking sheet. Brush the top of the pasties with the remaining beaten egg and bake in the preheated oven for 20 – 25 minutes until crisp and golden brown.

These deliciously different little pasties make great picnic food, and are also a great addition to children's lunchboxes.

Grilled Sausage Salad with Avocado, Blue Cheese, Onion and Tomato

Cook the sausages on a medium setting or on the barbecue until lightly browned, this should take 10 – 15 minutes. Cut into thick slices.

Mix the avocado, red onion and roughly chopped tomatoes into a bowl. To make the dressing, whisk together all of the ingredients until creamy, adjust the seasoning according to taste.

Place the salad leaves on 4 individual plates or large bowls, top with the sliced sausage then the avocado mixture and sprinkle with the blue cheese and croutons. Spoon the dressing over the salad leaves and garnish with the freshly chopped chives.

8 good quality pork sausages
1 ripe avocado, peeled, stoned and cut into chunks
1 red onion, peeled and finely chopped
4 tomatoes, roughly chopped
2 crisp lettuces such as Little Gem, leaves washed and torn into pieces
110g blue cheese, crumbled
3 tbsp bread croutons
2 tbsp chives, chopped
Sea salt and black pepper

For the dressing
6 tbsp rapeseed oil
1 tbsp Dijon mustard
1 clove garlic, peeled and crushed
1 tsp caster sugar
2 tsp red wine vinegar

Serves 4

Preheat barbecue/grill

Sausage, Sage and Onion Burgers with Spiced Apples and Sweet Potato Chips

First make the burgers, heat 1 tablespoon of the rapeseed oil in a small saucepan, add the onion and stir well. Cover and cook for 5 minutes, until the onion has softened, but do not allow to brown. Remove to a mixing bowl and leave to cool. Once cool, mix in the sausage meat, chopped sage and a little freshly ground black pepper. Mix well and form the mixture into 4 burger-shaped patties.

For the sweet potato chips, drizzle rapeseed oil over the sweet potatoes in a large bowl so that they are all well coated. Season with black pepper and place in a roasting tin. Roast in the preheated oven for 30 – 35 minutes until cooked through and golden brown around the edges. Season with sea salt and keep warm.

For the spiced apple wedges, melt the butter in a small frying pan. Add the apple wedges, spices, sugar, white wine vinegar and stir over a low heat until the apples are caramelised and soft, around 5 minutes.

Brush the sausage burgers with the remaining rapeseed oil and cook on a hot barbecue for 5 – 10 minutes on each side, until cooked through. Serve with the apple wedges and sweet potato chips.

These delicious sausage burgers with their spiced apple wedges, make a perfect dish for the last barbecue of summer, as the nights are starting to draw in. Serve the burgers in buns, grilled pitta breads or slices of toasted ciabatta.

3 tbsp rapeseed oil
1 onion,
peeled and very finely chopped
450g good quality sausage meat
3 tbsp fresh sage leaves,
finely chopped

For the sweet potato chips
4 sweet potatoes,
scrubbed and cut into wedges
2 tbsp rapeseed oil
Sea salt and black pepper

For the spiced apples
2 Cox's apples, peeled,
cored and cut into wedges
30g butter
½ tsp cinnamon
½ tsp mixed spice
1 tsp soft light brown sugar
½ tsp white wine vinegar

Serves 4

Preheat the oven to
180°C/350°F/Gas Mark 5

Preheat barbecue/grill

Sausages

Smoky Cocktail Sausage Kebabs with Tomato and Sour Cream Dip

Mix the ketchup, vinegar, sugar, paprika and thyme leaves in a small casserole dish and add the sausages, coat well. Season and cover, place in the fridge to marinate for an hour.

Meanwhile prepare the tomato and sour cream dip. Mix together the chopped tomatoes, lemon juice and sugar and season with sea salt and black pepper. Leave to stand for 15 minutes. Add the Worcestershire sauce, spring onions, and sour cream, mix together, season and refrigerate until required.

Place 3 sausages onto each skewer alternating with the peppers, apple and cherry tomatoes. Cook for 10 – 15 minutes either on a barbecue or under a preheated grill, turning regularly and coat with any remaining marinade.

Serve the kebabs with the tomato and sour cream dip, a mixed salad and pitta breads.

Soak the wooden skewers in cold water for 30 minutes to prevent them from burning.

3 tbsp tomato ketchup
2 tbsp malt vinegar
1 tbsp light brown sugar
½ tsp smoked paprika
1 tsp thyme leaves, finely chopped
Dash Worcestershire sauce
450g (30) cocktail sausages
18 cherry tomatoes
2 green peppers, deseeded and cut into 2cm dice
3 Cox's apples, cored and cut into dice
sea salt and black pepper

For the tomato and sour cream dip
1 tomato, finely chopped
Juice of ½ lemon
½ tsp caster sugar
Dash Worcestershire sauce
4 spring onions, trimmed and finely chopped
1 small tub sour cream
Sea salt and black pepper

Makes 10 kebabs

You will also need
10 wooden skewers

Sausages

Roasted Summer Vegetable Salad with Barbecued Sausages

2 red onions,
peeled and roughly sliced
225g small new potatoes, halved
2 tbsp thyme
2 tbsp rapeseed oil
2 courgettes, cut into 2cm dice
1 red pepper,
deseeded and diced
1 orange pepper,
deseeded and diced
2 cloves garlic,
peeled and crushed
1 sprig rosemary
12 cherry tomatoes, halved
55g pitted black olives
55g sun-dried tomatoes, diced
8 good quality pork sausages,
barbecued or grilled
Sea salt and black pepper

For the dressing
4 tbsp rapeseed oil
2 tbsp red wine vinegar
1 tsp Dijon mustard
Pinch cayenne pepper
A dash of honey
2 tbsp basil, roughly chopped
Squeeze lemon juice
Sea salt and black pepper

Preheat the oven to
200°C/400°F/Gas Mark 6

Preheat barbecue/grill

Arrange the potatoes and onions on a baking tray, sprinkle with the thyme, drizzle with the rapeseed oil and season with sea salt and black pepper. Bake in the preheated oven for 20 minutes, turning occasionally until browned and tender. Add the courgettes, peppers, garlic and rosemary and roast for a further 20 minutes. Add the cherry tomatoes and return to the oven for a further 5 minutes.

Meanwhile place the sausages on a preheated barbecue or grill and cook for 10 – 15 minutes, turning occasionally, until browned and thoroughly cooked.

To make the dressing, whisk together the rapeseed oil, vinegar, mustard, cayenne pepper, honey, basil and lemon juice in a bowl until creamy. Toss the diced sun-dried tomatoes and olives in the dressing and season to taste with sea salt and black pepper.

Arrange the roasted vegetables on a large platter and drizzle over the dressing. Serve with the barbecued sausages.

More sausages are
eaten on a ~~Saturday~~
than any other day

Sausages
for Children

Sticky Sausages and Fruity Coleslaw

1 tbsp soy sauce
2 tbsp tomato ketchup
1 tbsp Dijon mustard
1 tbsp light muscovado sugar
Zest and juice of 1 orange
8 good quality pork sausages

For the fruity coleslaw
30g sultanas
1 tbsp lemon juice
225g firm white cabbage,
finely shredded
1 red apple, cored and diced
2 spring onions, finely chopped
2 carrots, peeled and grated
2 tbsp mayonnaise
2 tbsp Greek yoghurt

Serves 4 – 6

Preheat the grill

Mix together the soy sauce, ketchup, mustard, sugar, orange zest and juice in a bowl and add the sausages. Mix well and set aside to marinade whilst preparing the coleslaw. Put the sultanas in a large bowl and sprinkle with lemon juice, add the shredded cabbage, apple, spring onion and carrots. Toss together and add the mayonnaise and Greek yoghurt, season as required and mix thoroughly to combine.

Grill the marinated sausages under a moderate heat for about 10 – 15 minutes, turning frequently until browned and cooked through; take care not to burn. Remove the sausages and allow to cool slightly before slicing thickly.

Serve the sticky sausages with the fruity coleslaw and toasted pitta breads.

Sausage Meatballs with Chinese Stir-Fried Vegetables

Roll the sausage meat into small meatballs. Place on a greased baking tray and drizzle with rapeseed oil, cook in the preheated oven for 10 – 15 minutes until golden brown, turning at least once.

Meanwhile, cook the noodles according to the packet instructions.

In a small bowl, mix together the soy sauce, tomato ketchup, Chinese five spice powder and honey. Heat the rapeseed oil in a wok or frying pan, add the garlic, carrot, red pepper, baby corn and ginger and stir fry for 4 minutes. Add the sugar snaps or peas and spring onions and cook for a further minute.

Drain the noodles, add to the vegetables and pour in the soy sauce mixture. Toss well and serve in bowls, topped with the sausage meatballs.

500g good quality pork sausage meat
250g medium egg noodles
4 tbsp soy sauce
Pinch Chinese five spice powder
1 tbsp tomato ketchup
2 tbsp clear honey
2 tbsp rapeseed oil
1 clove garlic, peeled and crushed
2 carrots, peeled and cut into thin sticks
1 red pepper, deseeded and thinly sliced
110g baby corn, halved lengthways
1 tbsp fresh ginger, peeled and grated
100g sugar snap peas or frozen peas
4 spring onions, finely sliced

Serves 4 – 6

Preheat the oven to 200°C/400°F/Gas Mark 6

Children often love Chinese flavours. Packed full of colourful, crunchy vegetables, this is a nutritious and very tasty dish.

Sausages

Pea, Sausage and Tomato Fusilli

Heat the rapeseed oil in a frying pan and cook the sausages over a medium heat for 7 – 8 minutes until brown and cooked. Bring a large pan of salted water to the boil and cook the fusilli pasta according to the packet instructions.

Heat the rapeseed oil in a saucepan and add the garlic. Cook for 30 seconds, then add the cherry tomatoes, chopped tomatoes, stock, sugar and basil. Bring to the boil and simmer for 10 minutes. Add the frozen peas and cook for a further 2 minutes.

Drain the pasta and thickly slice the cooked sausages, and add both into the sauce. Stir well so that the pasta is well coated with the sauce, and tip into an ovenproof dish. Sprinkle the grated Parmesan over the top and place in the preheated oven for 10 minutes, until the cheese has melted and the dish is bubbling. Serve with a salad and garlicky, cheesy bread.

1 tbsp rapeseed oil
4 good quality pork sausages
225g fusilli pasta
1 tbsp rapeseed oil
1 clove garlic,
peeled and crushed
110g cherry tomatoes, halved
1 x 400g tin peeled and
chopped tomatoes
75ml vegetable stock
½ tsp caster sugar
1 tbsp basil leaves, roughly torn
180g frozen peas
30g Parmesan cheese, grated

Serves 4

Preheat the oven to
200°C/400°F/Gas Mark 6

Sausages

Sausage and Pea Cakes

4 good quality pork sausages
500g potatoes,
peeled and cut into pieces
6 spring onions, finely chopped
30g butter
1 tsp English mustard (optional)
3 tbsp parsley, finely chopped
1 tbsp plain flour,
plus extra for shaping the cakes
100g frozen peas,
blanched and refreshed
1 egg yolk
3 tbsp rapeseed oil

Serves 4

Preheat the grill

Grill the sausages under a moderate heat for 10 – 15 minutes, turning regularly, until browned and cooked through; take care not to burn. Leave to cool, when cool chop into small pieces.

Bring a large pan of water to the boil, add the potatoes and cook for 20 minutes until soft and cooked through. Drain well and mash. Transfer to a large mixing bowl. Melt the butter in a frying pan and fry the spring onion for 1 minute until just starting to soften. Add to the potatoes with the mustard, parsley, flour and peas and mix. Add the egg yolk and chopped sausages and mix well. Season as required.

On a lightly floured surface shape the mixture into 8 rounds and dust with flour. Heat the rapeseed oil in a large frying pan and fry the cakes slowly for 5 minutes on each side until lightly browned.

Serve with homemade tomato ketchup (see Accompaniments).

Sausage and Carrot Casserole with Apple Gravy

Heat the rapeseed oil in a large casserole dish, add the sausages and brown well on all sides. Remove and set aside. Add the onion, carrot, bacon and leeks and cook for 10 – 15 minutes over a medium heat, until softened and starting to brown. Stir in the flour and cook for a further minute, then blend in the apple juice and stock. Bring to the boil, return the sausages to the pan, and simmer gently for 25 minutes.

Add the apple pieces and cook for a further 10 – 15 minutes, until they have softened. Stir in the mustard and sage and adjust the seasoning as necessary. Serve with creamy mashed potato.

1 tbsp rapeseed oil
8 good quality pork sausages
1 onion,
peeled and finely chopped
2 large carrots, peeled and diced
4 rashers streaky bacon, sliced
1 leek, washed, trimmed and
finely sliced
1 tbsp plain flour
200ml good quality apple juice
100ml chicken stock
2 Cox's apples,
peeled, cored and diced
½ tbsp wholegrain mustard
(optional)
1 tbsp sage, finely chopped

Serves 4

This quick and easy casserole can be prepared ahead and simply reheated when necessary. It makes a lovely warming meal for a cold day.

Sausages

Spicy Sausage Pizza with Mozzarella and Basil

Sift the flour, yeast and salt into a bowl, make a well in the centre and add the rapeseed oil. Mix the honey into the lukewarm water, pour the water into the well and mix into a dough, adding a little more water if there are any dry bits left in the bowl. Knead the dough on a lightly floured surface for 5 minutes until it starts to become smooth and shiny. Place the dough in a clean, lightly oiled bowl and cover with cling film. Leave in a warm place to rise for about one hour, until doubled in size.

Meanwhile grill the spicy sausages for 10 minutes under the preheated grill, turning occasionally until lightly browned on all sides and just cooked through. Remove, slice and set aside.

Next prepare the tomato sauce. Heat the rapeseed oil in a frying pan, add the garlic and fry for 30 seconds. Add the tomatoes and basil, season as required and simmer for 10 minutes on a low heat. The sauce needs to be thick enough to spread on the pizza bases. Remove from the heat and allow to cool.

Place the dough on a lightly floured surface and knead for a further minute to remove any large pockets of air. Divide the dough in half and roll each piece out into a circle that is approximately 25cm / 10 inches in diameter. Finish stretching it with your hands, working from the centre to push the dough out; you want a thin-based pizza with slightly raised edges.

Now carefully lift the pizza dough onto two lightly greased baking sheets. Spread with the tomato sauce and top with the sliced sausage. Tear the mozzarella into pieces and scatter these over the pizzas with the basil leaves. Drizzle with rapeseed oil and bake in the preheated oven for 12 – 15 minutes until the crust is golden brown and the mozzarella is golden and bubbling. Serve with a crunchy green salad.

**4 spicy sausages,
grilled and sliced**
225g good quality mozzarella
20 fresh basil leaves
Rapeseed oil

For the pizza bases
**350g strong white flour,
plus extra for kneading**
2 tsp easy blend dried yeast
1 tsp sea salt
2 tbsp rapeseed oil
1 tsp clear honey
220ml lukewarm water

For the tomato sauce
2 tbsp rapeseed oil
**2 cloves garlic,
peeled and crushed**
2 x 400g tins plum tomatoes
Handful basil leaves, roughly torn

Serves 4

Preheat the oven to
220°C/425°F/Gas Mark 7

Preheat the grill

Baked Penne Pasta with Sausages, Sweetcorn and Cream Cheese

350g dried penne pasta
8 good quality pork sausages
2 tbsp rapeseed oil
1 small red onion, peeled and thinly sliced
250g cream cheese
1 tbsp mild wholegrain mustard
2 tbsp single cream
1 small tin sweetcorn, drained
110g Cheddar cheese, grated

Serves 4

Preheat the oven to
190°C/375°F/Gas Mark 5

Preheat the grill

Bring a large pan of salted water to the boil. Cook the pasta according to the packet instructions. Grill the sausages under the preheated grill for 10 – 15 minutes until golden brown and cooked through. Allow to cool slightly and slice thickly.

Meanwhile, heat the rapeseed oil in a frying pan, add the onion and fry gently for 5 – 10 minutes until soft. Drain the pasta well and return to the pan. Add the cream cheese, mustard, cream, onions, sliced sausages and sweetcorn and mix well. Place in an ovenproof dish, sprinkle with the Cheddar cheese and cook in the preheated oven for 15 minutes, until golden brown and bubbling.

Use light cream cheese for a low-fat version of this dish.

Sausages with Homemade Chunky Chips and Spicy Relish

Wash the potatoes, dry well and cut them into thick chunky chips. Toss in the rapeseed oil, season with sea salt and black pepper, spread out on a baking sheet and bake for 45 minutes, turning from time to time.

Meanwhile, grill the sausages under a moderate heat for 10 – 15 minutes, turning regularly, until browned and cooked through, take care not to burn.

Whilst the chips and sausages are cooking prepare the spicy relish. Mix together the tomatoes, cucumber, chilli, red onion, garlic, sugar, rapeseed oil, lime juice, coriander and season with sea salt & black pepper.

Serve the relish with the sausages and homemade chunky chips.

8 good quality pork sausages
450g potatoes
2 – 3 tbsp rapeseed oil

For the spicy relish
4 tomatoes, finely diced
½ cucumber, finely diced
1 red chilli,
deseeded and very finely sliced
½ red onion,
peeled and finely diced
1 clove garlic,
peeled and crushed
1 tsp light brown sugar
2 tbsp rapeseed oil
1 tbsp lime juice
2 tbsp coriander, finely chopped
Sea salt and black pepper

Serves 4

Preheat oven to
200°C/400°F/Gas Mark 6

Preheat the grill

Sausages

Queen Victoria preferred the meat in her sausage to be chopped rather than minced

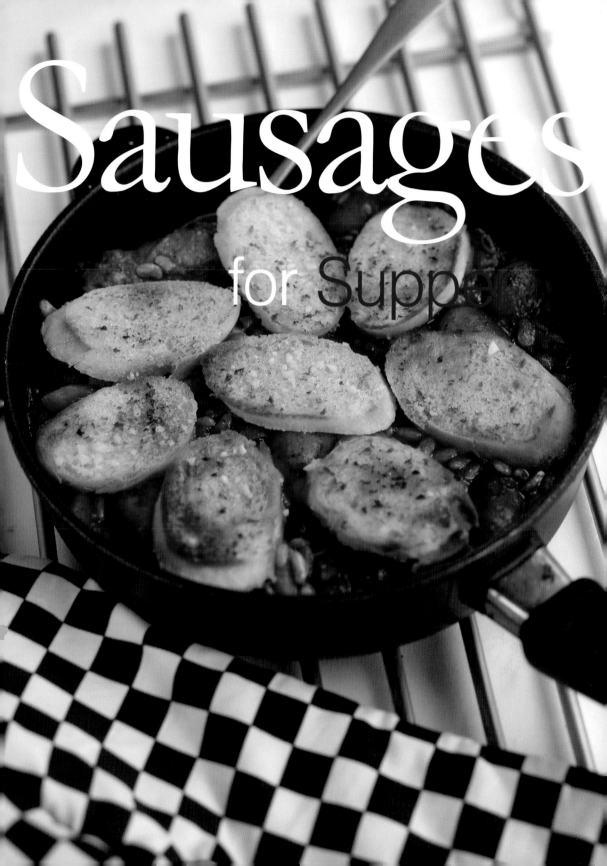

Sausages

for Supper

Sausage and Flageolet Bean Casserole with Garlic Crostini

8 good quality pork sausages
1 tbsp rapeseed oil
8 shallots, peeled and left whole
1 carrot, peeled and diced
1 stick celery, diced
1 clove garlic,
peeled and crushed
1 sprig rosemary
1 bay leaf
100ml white wine
150ml chicken stock
250g fresh
or tinned flageolet beans
2 x 400g tins chopped tomatoes
1 tbsp redcurrant jelly
50g black olives, pitted
1 tbsp parsley, finely chopped
Sea salt and black pepper

For the garlic crostini
8 slices baguette
55g butter, softened
2 cloves garlic,
peeled and crushed

Serves 4

Preheat grill

Heat the rapeseed oil in a heavy based pan or casserole and brown the sausages on all sides. Remove from the pan and reserve. Add the shallots, carrots and celery to the pan and sauté for 5 minutes, then add the garlic, rosemary and bay leaf and cook for a further minute.

Add the wine and stock, bring to the boil, then add the flageolet beans, tomatoes and redcurrant jelly. Return the sausages to the pan and simmer for 30 – 40 minutes, until the sauce has thickened and the beans are soft and cooked through. Add the olives and cook for a further 5 minutes. Check the seasoning, remembering the olives are salty, and adjust as necessary.

For the crostini, mix together the crushed garlic and softened butter and season with sea salt and black pepper. Spread the garlic butter onto both sides of the baguette slices and grill each side until golden.

Sprinkle the parsley over the casserole and serve with the garlic crostini.

Sausages Braised with Cider, Apples and Mustard

Heat half the butter in a casserole or sauté pan. Fry the sausages over a medium heat until they are well browned on all sides. Remove and set aside. Add the remaining butter to the pan and add the shallots. Cook for 5 minutes, until the shallots have started to soften, then add the apple and sauté for a minute.

Add the flour and stir well to make a roux. Blend in the cider and bring to the boil. Boil for 2 minutes, then turn down to a simmer and add the cream and mustard. Season to taste with sea salt and black pepper and return the sausages to the pan. Cook over a gentle heat for 10 minutes, until the sausages are cooked through. Sprinkle with the chopped parsley and serve.

55g butter
8 good quality pork sausages
2 shallots,
peeled and finely chopped
2 eating apples,
peeled, cored and diced
20g plain flour
150ml dry cider
150ml double cream
1 tbsp wholegrain mustard
1 tbsp parsley, finely chopped
Sea salt and black pepper

Serves 4

Sausages

Sausages with Red Cabbage and Pears

Melt the rapeseed oil with the butter in a large ovenproof casserole, add the onions, cover and cook over a low heat until soft but not brown. Add the shredded cabbage, garlic, cinnamon stick, cloves, coriander seeds, nutmeg, sugar and red wine vinegar and season well.

Cover the casserole with a tight lid and cook in the preheated oven for one hour, stirring occasionally. Add the prunes, pears and port and cook for a further 45 minutes, adding a little water if the cabbage becomes dry.

Meanwhile grill the sausages under the preheated grill for 10 – 15 minutes, or until cooked. Take the cabbage out of the oven, adjust the seasoning and serve with the sausages.

2 tbsp rapeseed oil
55g butter
1 onion, peeled and sliced
½ red cabbage, shredded, discarding the hard stalk
1 clove garlic, peeled and crushed
1 cinnamon stick
½ tsp ground cloves
6 crushed coriander seeds
Pinch nutmeg, grated
2 tbsp soft light brown sugar
3 tbsp red wine vinegar
55g pitted prunes, finely diced
2 large pears, peeled, cored and cut into eighths
2 tbsp port
Sea salt and black pepper
8 good quality pork sausages

Preheat oven to 150°C/300°F/Gas Mark 2

Preheat the grill

Red cabbage is often served with apple, but pears make a delicious alternative.

Sausages Wrapped in Bacon with Ratatouille and Cannellini Beans

8 good quality pork sausages
8 rashers streaky bacon
1 tbsp rapeseed oil

For the ratatouille
6 tbsp rapeseed oil
1 onion, peeled and finely sliced
4 cloves garlic,
peeled and crushed
2 red peppers, deseeded
and cut into 2cm chunks
1 strip orange peel
½ tsp caster sugar
1 x 400g tin chopped tomatoes
1 aubergine, cut into 2cm chunks
2 courgettes,
cut into 2cm chunks
1 x 300g tin cannellini beans,
drained and rinsed
Sea salt and black pepper
A handful of chopped basil leaves

Serves 4

First make the ratatouille. Heat 3 tablespoons of the rapeseed oil in a large pan or casserole. Add the onions, garlic and peppers along with the strip of orange peel. Cook on a medium heat for 10 minutes, stirring from time to time, until the vegetables have softened. Add the sugar and season with sea salt and black pepper, cook for a further 2 minutes, then add the tomatoes and bring to the boil. Season well and turn down to a gentle simmer. Meanwhile, heat the remaining rapeseed oil in a large frying pan and sauté the aubergine and courgettes until lightly browned. Add to the ratatouille, check the seasoning and simmer for a further 10 minutes.

While the ratatouille is cooking, wrap each sausage in a rasher of streaky bacon and grill or fry in the rapeseed oil until golden brown and cooked through, around 10 – 15 minutes. Add the cannellini beans to the ratatouille, stir well and heat through. Remove the strip of orange peel and discard. Adjust the seasoning and stir in the basil leaves.

Serve the bacon-wrapped sausages with the ratatouille.

Glazed Honey Mustard Sausages with Crushed Colcannon

Mix the oil, honey and mustard together in a large bowl, add the sausages and coat thoroughly. Line a roasting tin with a double layer of foil and lightly oil it. Tip in the sausages, arrange in a single layer and cook in the preheated oven for 20 – 25 minutes, turning regularly, until golden brown and sticky.

Meanwhile, cook the potatoes in a pan of boiling, salted water for 15 minutes, until tender. In a separate pan, blanch the shredded cabbage for 2 minutes, then drain and refresh.

Melt the butter with the rapeseed oil in a frying pan and add the onion and bacon. Cook for 5 – 10 minutes, until the onion has softened and both are lightly golden. Add the garlic and cook for a further minute. Drain the potatoes well and crush roughly with a fork, stir in the blanched cabbage, the buttery onion, bacon and garlic mixture. Pour in the cream, mix together well and cook over a medium heat for a couple of minutes until piping hot. Season with sea salt and black pepper and serve with the glazed honey mustard sausages.

1 tbsp rapeseed oil
1 tbsp runny honey
2 tbsp wholegrain mustard
8 good quality pork sausages
750g potatoes,
peeled and cut into quarters
½ savoy cabbage, outer leaves
removed, finely shredded
75g butter
1tbsp rapeseed oil
1 onion,
peeled and finely chopped
4 rashers streaky bacon,
chopped
1 clove garlic,
peeled and crushed
2 tbsp double cream
Sea salt and black pepper

Serves 4

Preheat the oven to
180°C/350°F/Gas Mark 4

Sausages

Sausage Meatballs with Sage and Spaghetti Carbonara

In a bowl mix the sausage meat together well with the breadcrumbs, chopped sage, black pepper and the beaten egg. Form the mixture into little meatballs.

Heat a large frying pan and add a good splash of oil, fry the meatballs until brown all over. Cook gently for a further 5 minutes and remove, keep warm. Fry the bacon for a couple of minutes, add the mushrooms and sauté for a further 2 minutes, add the garlic and remove from the heat.

Meanwhile, bring a large pan of salted water to the boil, add the spaghetti, stir well and cook for 10 – 12 minutes or until al dente.

Mix together the egg yolks, cream and half of the mature Cheddar cheese, lemon zest and parsley. When the pasta is cooked, drain, reserving a little of the cooking water and immediately toss it with the egg mixture, place back in the pasta pan and then add the meatball mixture. This should be enough heat to cook the egg mixture without scrambling it, if the mixture is a little sticky add some of the reserved cooking liquor, to loosen the mixture. Mix together. Sprinkle with the rest of the cheese.

Eat with green salad and chunky bread and crispy chards of streaky bacon.

500g good quality sausage meat
55g breadcrumbs
2 tbsp sage, finely chopped
3 large egg yolks
1 tbsp rapeseed oil
4 rashers streaky bacon, sliced
110g mushrooms, cut into slices
3 cloves garlic,
peeled and crushed
450g dried spaghetti
1 whole egg, beaten
150ml single cream
Zest of 1 lemon
150g Parmesan or
mature Cheddar cheese, grated
3 tbsp flat leaf parsley,
finely chopped
Sea salt and black pepper

Serves 6 – 8

Oven-Baked Sausages with Prunes and Walnut and Lemon Gremolata

2 red onions,
peeled and finely sliced
110g ready to eat prunes
2 bay leaves
2 sprigs thyme
2 tbsp rapeseed oil
8 good quality pork sausages
290ml red wine
50ml crème de cassis
(blackcurrant liqueur)
Sea salt and black pepper

For the gremolata
1 lemon, zested
2 cloves garlic,
peeled and finely chopped
2 tbsp flat leaf parsley,
finely chopped
30g walnuts,
lightly toasted and finely chopped

Serves 4

Preheat the oven to
190°C/375°F/Gas Mark 5

Place the sliced onions, prunes, bay leaves and thyme in the base of a large ovenproof dish. Season with sea salt and black pepper and drizzle over 1 tablespoon of the rapeseed oil. Toss together so that the onions and prunes are coated in the oil. Lay the sausages on top in a single layer and drizzle with the remaining oil. Mix together the red wine and crème de cassis and pour around the sausages. Roast in the preheated oven for 30 – 40 minutes, turning the sausages occasionally to ensure that they colour evenly. Make sure the prunes are not on top or they will burn. When the sausages are cooked the sauce should be reduced and slightly sticky.

Meanwhile mix all the gremolata ingredients in a bowl and set aside.

Serve the sausages and sauce with plenty of creamy mashed potato (see Accompaniments), and sprinkle with the gremolata.

The gremolata brings a lovely freshness to this sweet and sticky dish. Toasting the walnuts really brings out their flavour, but make sure you allow them to cool before mixing with the other ingredients.

Sausages Cooked in Beer

Heat the butter with 1 tablespoon of the rapeseed oil in a large, heavy bottomed casserole. Add the onions and carrots, stir well, cover and cook for 10 minutes. Add the celeriac and garlic and cook for a further 5 minutes, then add the sugar, increase the heat and caramelise the vegetables.

Meanwhile bring the beef stock to the boil in a separate pan and boil rapidly until it is reduced by half. Pan fry or grill the sausages, using the remaining oil if pan frying, until brown on all sides.

Add the flour to the vegetables and cook for a minute, then stir in the tomato purée. Blend in the beer and reduced stock and bring to the boil. Boil for 2 minutes then reduce the heat and add the browned sausages. Add the balsamic vinegar and redcurrant jelly and simmer gently for 10 – 15 minutes. Adjust the seasoning as necessary, sprinkle with the chopped parsley and serve.

30g butter
2 tbsp rapeseed oil
2 onions,
peeled and finely chopped
2 carrots, peeled and diced
110g celeriac, peeled and diced
1 clove garlic,
peeled and crushed
½ tbsp caster sugar
290ml beef stock
8 good quality pork sausages
20g plain flour
2 tsp tomato purée
250ml beer
½ tbsp balsamic vinegar
½ tbsp redcurrant jelly
1 tbsp parsley, finely chopped
Sea salt and black pepper

Serves 4

Sausages are mentioned in The Odyssey which was written by Homer more than 2,700 years ago

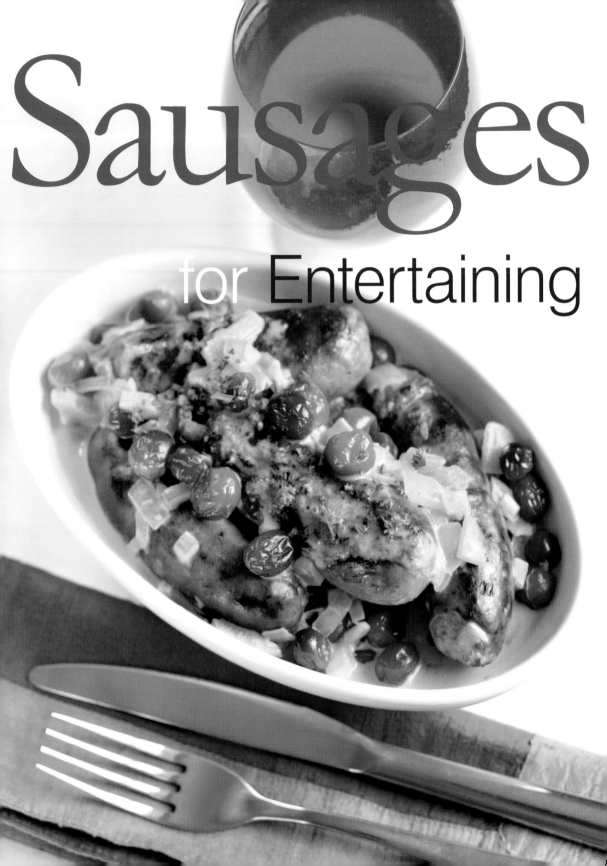

Sausages

for Entertaining

Moroccan Lamb Sausages and Chick Peas with Toasted Almond Couscous

3 tbsp rapeseed oil
1 onion,
peeled and finely chopped
3 cloves garlic,
peeled and crushed
1 tbsp fresh ginger,
peeled and grated
½ red chilli,
seeds removed, finely chopped
1 cinnamon stick
½ tsp turmeric
Pinch saffron threads
2 tsp ground cinnamon
2 tsp coriander seeds, crushed
4 tbsp fresh coriander,
finely chopped
8 lamb sausages
1 x 400g tin chopped tomatoes
1 x 400g tin chick peas, drained,
rinsed and partially crushed
1 tbsp honey
Zest and juice of 1 lemon
575ml good quality chicken stock
Sea salt and black pepper

For the couscous
3 tbsp rapeseed oil
1 red onion,
peeled and finely chopped
½ tsp ground cinnamon
½ tsp ground coriander
200g couscous
Juice and rind of 1 lemon
2 tbsp blanched almonds,
toasted and roughly chopped
3 tbsp coriander, finely chopped

Serves 4

Preheat the oven to
140°C/275°F/Gas Mark 1

Heat 2 tablespoons of the rapeseed oil in a large casserole or heavy saucepan over a medium heat. Add the onions, garlic, ginger, chilli and spices and season with sea salt and black pepper. Cook, covered, on a low heat for 5 minutes until the onions are soft. In a separate pan heat the remaining oil and brown the sausages well on all sides.

Add the chopped tomatoes, chick peas, honey, lemon zest and juice and chicken stock to the onions. Bring to the boil, cover and turn down to a gentle simmer for 30 minutes, then add the lamb sausages and cook for a further 10 – 15 minutes.

Meanwhile prepare the couscous. Heat the rapeseed oil in an ovenproof casserole. Add the onion and spices and sauté for 2 – 3 minutes. Remove from the heat and add the couscous, mixing well so that it is coated with the onion and spice mixture. Pour over 400ml of boiling water, season, cover and place the couscous in the preheated oven for 5 minutes.

Remove the couscous from the oven and fluff up the grains with a fork. Squeeze over the lemon juice, scatter with the chopped, toasted almonds and coriander and serve with the lamb sausages.

Warm Sausage, Fig and Goat's Cheese Salad in a Balsamic and Lemon Dressing

Cook the sausages under the preheated grill for 10 – 15 minutes, turning occasionally until browned on all sides and cooked through. Thickly slice and keep warm.

Preheat a griddle pan. Slice the fennel in half and remove the tough outer parts of the bulb. Cut each half lengthways into 3 pieces, place in a bowl with the peppers and figs and add the rapeseed oil. Season with sea salt and black pepper and mix well so that all the vegetables are coated in the oil. Grill the fennel wedges on the hot griddle pan for 3 minutes each side, remove and keep warm, then griddle the peppers and figs for 2 minutes each side.

Meanwhile make the dressing. Whisk all the ingredients together, tear in the basil leaves and season with sea salt and black pepper. Whilst the fennel, peppers and figs are still warm place them in the dressing.

Grill the goats cheese rounds on a lightly greased baking sheet for 2 minutes or until the cheese begins to melt and brown on the top.

Wash and dry the salad leaves, divide between 4 large plates and top with the grilled vegetables and sausages. Scatter with the pine nuts and top with the grilled goat's cheese. Drizzle over any remaining dressing and serve.

8 good quality pork sausages
2 bulbs fennel
2 red peppers,
deseeded and diced
4 figs, halved lengthways
2 tbsp rapeseed oil
200g goat's cheese log,
cut into 4 rounds
2 good handfuls rocket,
watercress or
other peppery leaves
55g pine nuts, toasted

For the dressing
3 tbsp rapeseed oil
1 tbsp balsamic or fig vinegar
Juice and zest 1 lemon
10 fresh basil leaves

Serves 4

Preheat the grill

Black Pudding Sausages in a Winter Salad with Poached Eggs

Heat half the rapeseed oil in a frying pan and add the black pudding sausages and red pepper. Fry over a medium heat until browned and cooked. Remove from the pan and keep warm. Place the pan back on the heat and add the remaining oil. Shallow fry the bread cubes, turning to ensure they are brown all over. Sprinkle with the paprika and cook for a further 30 seconds.

For the dressing, heat the oil and add the garlic. Heat for 10 seconds. Add the red wine vinegar, mustard and pinch of sugar. Turn off the heat and keep warm.

Meanwhile poach 4 eggs and while doing this, put the sausage, pepper and salad leaves on a serving dish. Add the poached eggs and croutons, then dress the salad and garnish with chopped chives or parsley.

2 tbsp rapeseed oil
8 black pudding sausages,
cut into 1cm slices
1 red pepper,
deseeded and diced
2 thick slices crusty bread,
cut into 1 – 2cm cubes
½ tsp paprika
4 eggs
250g mixed salad leaves
Chives, finely chopped, to garnish

For the dressing
3 tbsp rapeseed oil
2 cloves garlic,
peeled and crushed
2 tbsp red wine vinegar
1 tsp Dijon mustard
Sea salt and black pepper
Pinch caster sugar

Serves 4

Sausages

Sausages with Gnocchi, Pumpkin, Sage and Cream

2 tbsp rapeseed oil
4 shallots,
peeled and finely chopped
350g pumpkin, peeled,
deseeded and cut into 3cm cubes
2 cloves garlic,
peeled and crushed
1 tbsp sage leaves,
finely chopped
50ml vegetable stock
50ml white wine
200ml double cream
8 good quality pork sausages
500g gnocchi
Sea salt and black pepper
Parmesan cheese, to serve

Serves 4

Heat 1 tablespoon of the rapeseed oil in a sauté pan over a medium heat. Add the shallot and pumpkin, cover and sweat until the pumpkin has started to soften, about 10 minutes, season.

Add the garlic and sage and cook for another 2 minutes, then add the vegetable stock and white wine and bring to the boil. Reduce the liquid by half, then add the double cream and simmer for 3 – 4 minutes, until thickened.

Meanwhile heat the remaining rapeseed oil in a pan and cook the sausages until golden brown and cooked through. Bring 2 litres of salted water to the boil, add the gnocchi, return to the boil and cook until all the gnocchi has risen to the surface, about 2 – 3 minutes. Drain well and add to the pumpkin sauce, along with the grated Parmesan cheese. Serve with the sausages and extra parmesan cheese (optional).

Fresh gnocchi is now widely available and is easy to cook. This would also work as a quick supper dish, without the sausages.

Italian-Style Sausages with Fennel Seeds, Chilli and Oregano, served with a Cheese Polenta

To make the sauce, heat half the rapeseed oil in a frying pan and add the red onions. Fry for 5 minutes, until the onion is soft but not browned, then add the fennel seeds, garlic and chilli and fry for a further minute. Add the tomatoes, stock and wine and stir in the oregano and parsley. Season, bring to the boil and simmer for 20 – 25 minutes, stirring occasionally.

For the polenta, place the stock, cream, garlic and thyme in a heavy based saucepan and bring to the boil. Remove from the heat and leave to infuse for 10 minutes.

Meanwhile, heat the remaining rapeseed oil over a medium heat and fry the sausages until well browned, about 8 – 10 minutes. Add to the tomato sauce and cook for a further 5 minutes.

To finish the polenta, remove the garlic and thyme and bring the liquid back to the boil. Stir in the polenta and cook over a low heat, whisking constantly for 6 – 8 minutes until thick. Stir in the butter and cheese and season with sea salt and black pepper.

Check the seasoning of the sausages and serve with the cheese polenta and some torn oregano leaves.

4 tbsp rapeseed oil
2 red onions,
peeled and finely chopped
1 tsp fennel seeds
2 cloves garlic,
peeled and crushed
½ red chilli,
deseeded and finely chopped
2 x 400g tins
premium Italian tinned tomatoes
100ml vegetable stock
50ml white wine
1 tbsp oregano, finely chopped,
plus extra leaves to serve
1 tbsp parsley, finely chopped
8 good quality farmhouse
sausages with garlic
Sea salt and black pepper

For the cheese polenta
800ml good quality vegetable or
chicken stock
200ml double cream
2 garlic cloves,
peeled and lightly crushed
1 sprig thyme
200g quick cook polenta
110g Parmesan cheese
1 tbsp butter
Sea salt and black pepper

Serves 4

Venison Sausages with Roasted Garlic Mash

First prepare the garlic for the mash. Cut the head of garlic in half horizontally and place both halves, cut side up, on a sheet of tin foil. Drizzle with half of the rapeseed oil and season with sea salt and black pepper. Loosely wrap the foil over the top of the garlic to make a parcel and twist the edges to seal. Place on a baking sheet and roast in the preheated oven for 30 – 40 minutes, until the garlic is completely soft and lightly caramelised.

For the sausages, heat the rapeseed oil in a casserole dish or heavy based saucepan and brown the sausages well on all sides. Remove from the pan and set aside. Add the onion and cook over a low heat for 10 minutes until soft and translucent. Add the juniper berries and flour and cook for a further 2 minutes. Blend in the balsamic vinegar, red wine and stock, stirring all the time, until you have a smooth, thickened sauce. Add the redcurrant jelly and herbs and return the sausages to the pan. Simmer gently for 15 minutes.

For the mash, place the potatoes in a large pan of salted water and bring to the boil. Simmer until tender, drain very well and purée through a ricer for a very smooth texture. If you do not have a ricer just ensure that you mash the potatoes as smoothly as possible. Season well with sea salt and black pepper and squeeze in the roasted garlic cloves. Add the remaining rapeseed oil and beat in well. Serve with the sausages and sauce.

2 tbsp rapeseed oil
8 venison sausages
1 onion,
peeled and finely chopped
8 juniper berries
1 tbsp plain flour
1 tbsp balsamic vinegar
200ml red wine
300ml chicken / game stock
1 tbsp redcurrant jelly
1 bay leaf
½ tbsp thyme leaves

For the roasted garlic mash
1 head garlic
4 tbsp rapeseed oil
1kg floury potatoes,
peeled and cut into quarters
Sea salt and black pepper

Serves 4

Preheat the oven to
180°C/350°F/Gas Mark 4

Venison Sausages
with Sour Cream and Cranberries

Heat the rapeseed oil in a casserole dish or heavy-based pan and fry the sausages until well browned and cooked through, about 10 – 12 minutes. Set aside.

Melt the butter and add the onion. Cook for 10 – 15 minutes, stirring from time to time, until completely softened. Add the garlic and juniper berries and cook for a further minute. Add the white wine, cranberries and cranberry sauce and return the sausages to the pan. Bring to the boil and simmer for 5 minutes, until the liquid has reduced and the cranberries have softened slightly. Season to taste.

Stir in the soured cream, being careful not to let the sauce boil as this will cause the cream to curdle. Sprinkle with the chopped parsley and serve with mashed potatoes.

1 tbsp rapeseed oil
8 venison sausages
20g butter
1 onion, peeled and finely sliced
1 clove garlic,
peeled and crushed
4 juniper berries, crushed
50ml white wine
110g fresh cranberries
2 tbsp cranberry sauce
150ml sour cream
1 tbsp chopped parsley
Sea salt and black pepper

Serves 4

Venison sausages are a little bit special, and the use of cranberries make this a perfect meal for serving over the festive period. If making ahead, don't add the sour cream until just before serving.

Sausages in Red Wine with Bacon and Thyme, with Creamed Celeriac

2 tbsp rapeseed oil
8 good quality pork sausages
4 rashers streaky bacon
1 onion,
peeled and finely chopped
150g button mushrooms, wiped
45g dried porcini mushrooms,
soaked in warm water
2 cloves garlic,
peeled and crushed
1 tbsp plain flour
1 bay leaf
6 juniper berries, crushed
2 sprigs thyme
200ml red wine
75ml port
1 x 400g tin chopped
plum tomatoes
½ tbsp tomato ketchup
1 tbsp redcurrant jelly

For the creamed celeriac
1 celeriac,
peeled and roughly chopped
300g potatoes,
peeled and cut into quarters
55g butter, melted
2 tbsp double cream
Pinch celery salt
Sea salt and black pepper

Serves 4

Heat the rapeseed oil in a sauté pan or deep frying pan. Brown the sausages on all sides, remove from the pan and set aside. Add the bacon to the hot pan and cook until golden brown, then add the onion and cook for 5 minutes, stirring from time to time. Add the mushrooms and cook for a further 2 minutes until they are just soft.

Then add the garlic, flour, bay leaf, juniper berries, porcini mushrooms and thyme and cook, stirring, for a minute. Pour in the red wine and bring to a simmer. Add the tinned tomatoes, tomato ketchup and redcurrant jelly, and return the sausages to the pan. Season to taste, turn down to a simmer, cover and cook for 15 – 20 minutes, until the sauce has thickened and reduced slightly.

Meanwhile prepare the creamed celeriac. Cook the celeriac and potatoes in boiling salted water for 20 minutes, until soft. Drain well and mash thoroughly. Add the butter, cream and celery salt and season to taste.

Pile the creamed celeriac into a bowl and serve with the sausages.

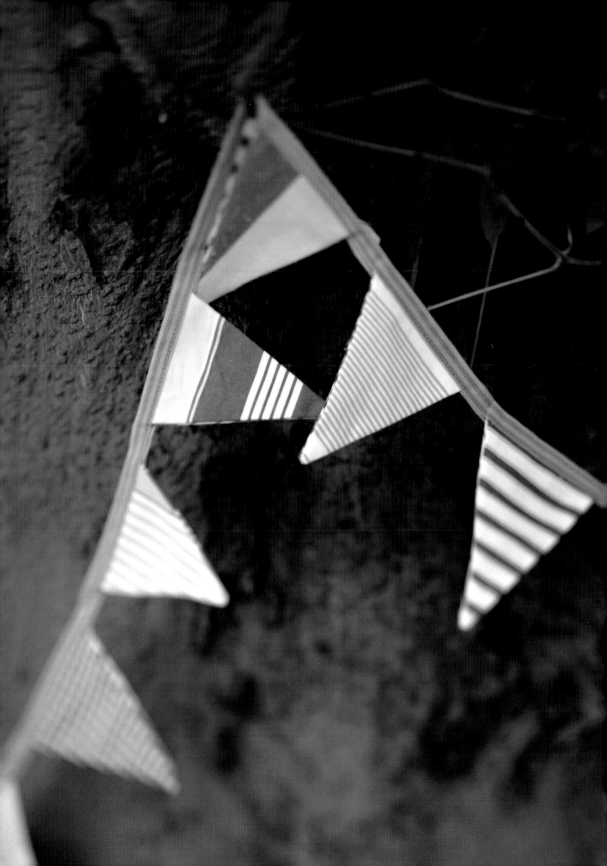

In the last year
182,848 tonnes
of sausages were
consumed in the UK

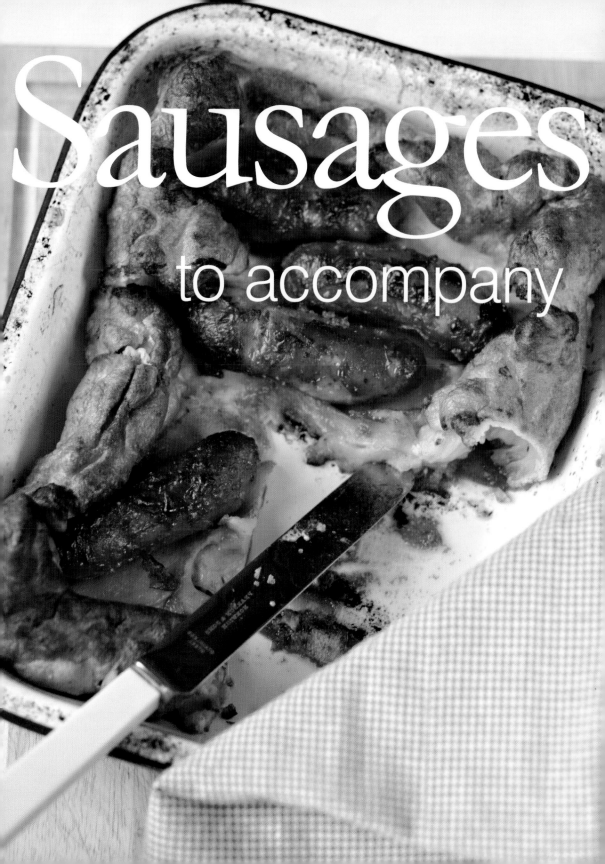

Sausages

to accompany

Stir-Fried Cabbage with Cardamom

1 medium Savoy cabbage
12 cardamom pods
4 tbsp rapeseed oil
55g butter
2 cloves garlic,
peeled and crushed
sea salt and black pepper

Serves 4

Cut the cabbage into quarters, discarding any tough outer leaves. Remove the core from each quarter, then finely shred. Crush the cardamom pods with the flat blade of the knife, or in a pestle and mortar, to remove the seeds.

Heat the rapeseed oil and butter in a wok or large frying pan. Add the cabbage, you may have to do this in two batches. Stir-fry over a high heat, keeping the cabbage moving round the pan so that it does not catch. Add the cardamom seeds and cook until the cabbage is bright green and just tender. Add the garlic and stir-fry for a further 30 seconds, season to taste and serve.

Cheddar Mash

Boil the potatoes in a large pan of salted water until tender to the point of a knife. Drain very well and return to the hot pan. Mash thoroughly or put the potatoes through a ricer.

Over a very low heat, add the butter and cream and beat in well. Remove from the heat and stir in the grated Cheddar. Season to taste and serve.

**750g potatoes,
peeled and cut into pieces
55g butter
50ml double cream
100g mature Cheddar cheese,
finely grated
Sea salt and black pepper**

Serves 4

This rich dish makes a great accompaniment to some plain grilled or roasted sausages, and is popular with children. Add the cheese off the heat to ensure that it doesn't go stringy.

Perfect Mashed Potato

Cut the potatoes into even-sized pieces and place in a large pan of salted water. Bring to the boil and simmer until tender, around 20 – 25 minutes. Drain the potatoes well, return them to the saucepan and shake over a low heat for 30 seconds to remove some of the steam.

Heat the butter, milk and cream in a separate saucepan until the butter is just melted. Mash the potatoes with a masher and add the butter mixture, mixing in well until creamy and fluffy.

Season to taste with nutmeg, sea salt and black pepper.

**1kg potatoes, peeled and washed
(King Edward, Desirée or Maris Piper)
110g butter
2 tbsp whole milk
2 tbsp double cream
Pinch nutmeg
Sea salt and black pepper**

Serves 4 – 6

Sausages

Garlic Mash

1 whole garlic
4 tbsp rapeseed oil
1 kg floury potatoes,
peeled and cut into quarters
Sea salt and black pepper

Serves 4

Preheat the oven to
180°C/350°F/Gas Mark 4

First prepare the garlic. Cut the head of garlic in half horizontally and place both halves, cut side up, on a sheet of tin foil. Drizzle with half of the rapeseed oil and season with sea salt and black pepper. Loosely wrap the foil over the top of the garlic to make a parcel and twist the edges to seal. Place on a baking sheet and roast in the preheated oven for 30 – 40 minutes, until the garlic is completely soft and lightly caramelised.

Place the potatoes in a large pan of salted water and bring to the boil. Simmer until tender, drain very well and mash to a smooth texture, squeeze in the roasted garlic, add the remaining rapeseed oil and beat in well. Season with sea salt and black pepper.

Roasted garlic is deliciously sweet and nutty tasting and has many uses. Store the roasted garlic in a kilner jar covered with rapeseed oil, and you can use the flavoured oil as well. Great in pasta dishes, risottos and bruschetta.

Coriander and Tomato Salsa

Quarter and deseed the tomatoes, then chop into even sized dice, mix with the red onion, coriander, rapeseed oil and lime juice, season well with sea salt and black pepper. The salsa is improved be being made an hour or so in advance, to allow the flavours to develop.

Never over-mix a salsa as the flavours need to stay separate in your mouth!

4 ripe tomatoes
½ red onion,
peeled and finely chopped
Handful coriander, washed,
dried and roughly chopped
3 tbsp rapeseed oil
1 tbsp lime juice
Lime wedges, to garnish
Sea salt and black pepper

Serves 4

This fresh and summery salsa makes a great accompaniment to barbecued sausages. It would also go well with any barbecued meat or fish.

Sausages

Potato Wedges

Cut the potatoes lengthways into even-sized wedges and toss with the rapeseed oil in a large roasting tin. Season with sea salt and black pepper and roast in the preheated oven for 25 – 30 minutes, checking regularly and stirring to ensure that the potatoes do not stick.

500g potatoes, peeled
2 tbsp rapeseed oil
Sea salt and black pepper

Serves 4

Preheat the oven
220°C/425°F/Gas Mark 7

Sausages

Pea and Potato Cakes

1 large potato, peeled and cut
into large pieces
55g butter
1 onion,
peeled and finely chopped
110g smoked streaky bacon,
finely diced
55g plain flour
1 egg, beaten
100ml double cream
110g frozen peas, blanched
55g Cheddar cheese, grated
Sea salt and black pepper

Serves 4

Place the potato in a large pan of salted water and bring to the boil. Boil for 15 – 20 minutes, until tender. Drain well, mash thoroughly and allow to cool.

Melt half the butter and fry the onion and bacon until softened and golden brown. In a large bowl mix together the mashed potato with the flour, beaten egg and double cream. Add the onion and bacon mixture, the blanched peas and the grated Cheddar. Season to taste and mix well. Shape the mixture into cakes.

Melt the remaining butter in a frying pan and fry the cakes for 2 – 3 minutes on each side over a medium heat, until golden brown. Serve with sausages and a good quality tomato ketchup or chutney.

These Pea and Potato Cakes are great for children, and can easily be adjusted for vegetarians, just leave out the bacon.

Crushed Colcannon

Cook the potatoes in a large pan of boiling salted water for approximately 20 minutes. Cut the halved Savoy cabbage into quarters and remove the core. Finely shred the cabbage and blanch for 1 minute in a separate pan of boiling salted water. Drain well and refresh under cold water, then drain again.

When the potatoes are tender to the point of a knife drain them well, return them to the hot pan and keep warm. Melt the butter with the rapeseed oil in a large frying pan and add the onion and bacon. Fry until soft and lightly golden, then add the garlic and cook for a further minute. Add the potatoes, crush them lightly with a fork and mix well. Add the blanched cabbage and cook for a further 2 – 3 minutes, season well and serve.

750g potatoes,
peeled and cut into quarters
75g butter
1 tbsp rapeseed oil
½ Savoy cabbage
1 onion,
peeled and finely chopped
1 clove garlic crushed (optional)
4 rashers streaky bacon,
cut into small dice
2 tbsp double cream
Sea salt and black pepper

Serves 4

Barbecue Sauce

1 onion,
peeled and finely chopped
2 cloves garlic,
peeled and crushed
1 tbsp rapeseed oil
1 tsp black mustard seeds
1 tsp ground ginger
55ml soy sauce
2 tbsp maple syrup
1 tbsp red wine vinegar
300ml good quality tomato ketchup
Dash Tabasco sauce

Heat the rapeseed oil in a large saucepan, add the onion, garlic, mustard seeds and ground ginger and fry gently until the onion is soft but not browned. Add the soy sauce, maple syrup, red wine vinegar, ketchup and tabasco (according to taste) and season with sea salt and black pepper.

Bring to the boil, turn down and simmer for 5 minutes to combine the flavours.

Use this as an accompaniment or dip at a barbecue, or to marinade sausages and other meats prior to cooking. If you don't happen to have any maple syrup just substitute with 55g soft light brown sugar.

Warm Fig and Mustard Seed Chutney

Heat the rapeseed oil in a large, wide pan and add the onion. Sauté for 5 – 10 minutes, until softened, then add the figs, apples, ginger, mustard seeds, spices, salt, vinegar and lemon juice. Bring to the boil, stirring, and boil for 10 minutes.

Add the sugar and stir to dissolve. Simmer for 20 – 30 minutes, stirring occasionally, until the chutney has thickened. Spoon into sterilised jars, seal and label. The chutney will keep in a cool, dark place for 6 months.

1 tbsp rapeseed oil
2 large onions,
peeled and finely chopped
200g dried, ready-to-eat figs,
finely chopped
500g Cox's apples,
peeled, cored and finely chopped
5cm piece fresh ginger,
peeled and finely chopped
2 tsp black mustard seeds
Pinch cinnamon
Pinch nutmeg
1 tsp sea salt
400ml cider vinegar
Juice of 1 lemon
400g soft light brown sugar

Makes approximately
1kg of chutney

This wonderful chutney can be served warm or cold and is perfect with sausages in the winter months. It is also good with cheese or cold cuts of meat.

Roasted Sweet Potato, Shallot and Beetroot

3 cloves garlic,
peeled and crushed
2 tsp root ginger, grated
2 lemongrass sticks,
peeled and chopped
1 tbsp chopped mint
Handful coriander,
plus extra to garnish
2 tbsp sweet chilli sauce
2 tbsp honey
2 large sweet potatoes,
peeled and cut into 2cm cubes
2 red peppers,
deseeded cut into 2cm pieces
16 shallots, peeled and left whole
2 red onions,
peeled and quartered
4 uncooked beetroot,
peeled and quartered
4 tbsp rapeseed oil
Sea salt and black pepper

Serves 4 – 6

Preheat the oven to
200°C/400°F/Gas Mark 6

In a food processor, blend together the garlic, ginger, lemongrass, mint, coriander, sweet chilli sauce and honey. Season well.

Place the vegetables, apart from the peppers, in a large roasting tin, drizzle with the rapeseed oil and season with salt and pepper. Mix the vegetables well so that they are evenly coated with the oil. Roast for 25 minutes, then remove from the oven add the peppers and pour over the mixture and stir well. Place back in the oven. Roast for 15 – 20 minutes until nicely glazed. Garnish with the coriander and serve.

Peas with Chives and Rocket

Melt the butter in a large pan, add the shallots and cook over a medium heat for 3 – 4 minutes or until the shallots are soft but not coloured.

Pour in the vegetable stock, add a pinch of caster sugar, bring to the boil and season with sea salt and black pepper. Add the peas and cook for 3 – 5 minutes until cooked through. Stir in the rocket, crème fraiche and chives and cook for a further 2 minutes, check the seasoning and serve immediately.

55g butter
2 shallots,
peeled and finely chopped.
110ml vegetable stock
Pinch caster sugar
400g frozen peas
100g rocket leaves
2 tbsp crème fraiche
4 tbsp chives, finely chopped
Sea salt and black pepper

Serves 4 – 6

This light summery dish makes a perfect accompaniment to simple grilled or barbecued sausages, along with some boiled new potatoes.

Red Onion and Rosemary Jam

1kg red onions,
peeled and finely sliced
4 tbsp rapeseed oil
110g butter
150g caster sugar
150ml red wine
150ml red wine vinegar
2 tbsp port
2 sprigs rosemary
Sea salt and black pepper

Makes approximately
500g of jam

Heat the rapeseed oil and butter in a large saucepan. Add the onions and sugar and stir until well coated in the butter.

Reduce the heat and cook the onions for 10 minutes, stirring occasionally, until soft and just beginning to caramelise. Pour in the red wine, vinegar and port, add the rosemary and season with sea salt and black pepper. Simmer for 10 minutes until the onions are completely soft.

Remove from the heat, discard the rosemary sprigs and allow to cool. Use immediately or seal in sterilised jars. The jam will keep in the fridge for 2 weeks.

Sweet Piccalilli

Place the cauliflower, onions, vinegar, nutmeg and allspice in a large pan and bring to the boil. Cover and simmer for 8 minutes. Now take the lid off and stir in the cucumber, runner beans and sugar. Add the garlic and a teaspoon of salt. Bring the mixture up to simmering point again, cover and cook for a further 4 minutes. The vegetables should still be slightly crisp.

Drain the vegetables in a colander and reserve the liquid. Mix together the mustard powder, turmeric, ginger and flour in a bowl. Gradually mix in the cider vinegar and the 3 tablespoons of water until the mixture becomes a loose paste, stir and transfer to a saucepan. Bring to the boil, whisk and gradually add the hot reserved liquid. Simmer for 5 minutes. Place the vegetables in a large bowl and pour over the sauce. Stir well to mix then spoon into warmed, dry, screw top jars. Keep for 3 months in a cool, dark place before eating.

**2 cauliflowers,
broken into small florets
2 onions,
peeled and finely chopped
1 litre malt vinegar
½ tsp nutmeg
½ tsp allspice
1 cucumber,
cut into 1cm slices then quartered
450g runner beans, thickly sliced
340g caster sugar
3 cloves garlic,
peeled and finely chopped
1 tsp sea salt
3 tbsp English mustard powder
½ tbsp turmeric
1 tbsp ginger
5 tbsp plain flour
100ml cider vinegar
3 tbsp water**

Makes approximately
2kg of sweet piccalilli

Boozy Onion Gravy

30g butter
1 tbsp rapeseed oil
3 large onions,
peeled and finely sliced
3 sprigs thyme
1 bay leaf
1 tbsp plain flour
110ml red wine
75ml port
400ml fresh beef or chicken stock
½ tbsp balsamic vinegar
Dash Worcestershire sauce
Sea salt and black pepper

Serves 4

Melt the butter with the rapeseed oil in a frying pan. Add the onions, thyme and bay leaf and fry gently over a very low heat for about 20 minutes until soft. Increase the heat slightly and cook for a further 5 minutes, allowing the onions to brown and caramelise.

Add the flour and cook for 2 minutes, stirring constantly. Slowly add the wine and port, stirring all the time. Add the stock and simmer until reduced by a third. Season with the balsamic vinegar, Worcestershire sauce, sea salt and black pepper.

Serve immediately.

Homemade Tomato Ketchup

Place the tomatoes and onions in a large, heavy based saucepan over a gentle heat. Simmer very slowly, stirring occasionally, until the vegetables are very soft. Push the mixture through a sieve and return to the pan. Add the sugar, vinegar, garlic, tomato purée and mustard powder and stir well.

Place the allspice, cinnamon stick, bay leaf, cloves and peppercorns into a square of muslin, tie into a bundle with string and add to the pot. Bring the mixture to the boil, reduce to a slow simmer, and cook, stirring frequently, until the ketchup is quite thick; around 15 – 20 minutes.

Leave to cool, remove the muslin spice bag, season the ketchup with sea salt to taste and pour into sterilised bottles. Seal and store in the fridge.

1.5kg ripe tomatoes, roughly chopped
2 onions, peeled and finely sliced
110g soft light brown sugar
150ml white wine vinegar
1 clove garlic, peeled and crushed
1 tbsp tomato purée
1 tsp English mustard powder
½ tsp whole allspice
1 cinnamon stick
1 bay leaf
4 cloves
8 black peppercorns
Sea salt

Makes approximately 2kg of tomato ketchup

Sausages

Rhubarb, Ginger and Sweet Chilli Relish

500g rhubarb
2 shallots,
peeled and finely chopped
100ml cider vinegar
1cm piece fresh ginger,
peeled and finely chopped
200g soft light brown sugar
1 red chilli,
deseeded and finely chopped
Sea salt and black pepper

Wash and trim the rhubarb, then slice it into 2cm pieces. Place the shallots, cider vinegar, ginger and sugar in a pan and season with sea salt and black pepper. Bring to the boil for 5 minutes, then add the rhubarb and red chilli. Reduce the heat and simmer for 20 minutes or until slightly thickened.

If you are making the relish to use at a later date, you can put it in a sterilised jar whilst still hot and store in a cool, dark place.

This relish makes a fantastic dip for cocktail sausages served as a canapé. Make it with the early season forced rhubarb for a beautiful pink colour.

Cauliflower Cheese

To make the cheese sauce melt the butter, stir in the flour and cook over a low heat for 2 minutes, stirring constantly. Whisk in the milk and cream and continue to stir until the mixture is smooth. Simmer for 2 minutes and season to taste. Remove from the heat and stir in the mustard, Tabasco (if using) and grated Cheddar cheese.

Meanwhile, bring a pan of salted water to the boil and cook the cauliflower florets for 3 – 4 minutes. Drain well and set aside.

Melt the remaining butter in a frying pan and add the cauliflower florets. Toss them in the butter without allowing them to colour and season with sea salt and black pepper. Transfer the cauliflower to an ovenproof dish and top with the sauce, sprinkle with Parmesan cheese and breadcrumbs and bake for 15 – 20 minutes until golden brown.

40g butter
40g plain flour
400ml milk
175ml single cream
1 tsp English mustard
Dash Tabasco sauce (optional)
200g mature Cheddar cheese, grated
30g butter
1 cauliflower, divided into florets
30g Parmesan cheese
1 tbsp fresh breadcrumbs
Sea salt and black pepper

Serves 4

Preheat the oven to
190°C/375°F/Gas Mark 5

Butternut Squash and Apple Chutney

1.5kg butternut squash,
peeled and seeds removed
2 tbsp rapeseed oil
2 large onions,
peeled and finely chopped
1 tbsp fresh ginger,
peeled and grated
½ tbsp brown mustard seeds
½ tbsp cumin seeds
2 large cooking apples,
peeled, cored and diced
500g soft light brown sugar
750ml cider vinegar

Makes approximately
1kg of chutney

Cut the squash into 2cm pieces. Heat the rapeseed oil in a large pan and add the onions, ginger, mustard seeds and cumin seeds. Fry on a gentle heat for 5 minutes, stirring occasionally, until soft but not browned.

Add the squash and the rest of the ingredients and bring to the boil. Reduce the heat and simmer gently, uncovered, for about 45 – 60 minutes or until the chutney has thickened.

Serve warm, or seal in sterilised jars. The chutney can be stored in a cool, dry place for up to 6 months.

Index

Practical Stuff

All recipes
serve 4 unless otherwise stated

All recipes
specify 2 sausages per person, for
hungry families simply increase the
number of sausages

All measurements
are metric, use the charts opposite
for conversion to imperial

All eggs
are medium sized and free range

All teaspoon and tablespoon
measurements are level

Metric Conversion Scales

Oven temperature scales

°C	°F	Gas Mark
110°C	225°F	¼
130	250	½
140	275	1
150	300	2
170	325	3
180	350	4
190	375	5
200	400	6
220	425	7
230	450	8
240	475	9

Weight conversions

Grams	Ounces
30g	1oz
55g	2oz
85g	3oz
110g	4oz
150g	5oz
180g	6oz
200g	7oz
225g	8oz
250g	9oz
275g	10oz
315g	11oz
350g	12oz
375g	13oz
400g	14oz

1kg is equal to 2.2lb

Liquid conversions

Metric	Imperial	Fl oz
5ml	1 tsp	
15ml	1 tbsp	
25ml		1fl oz
75ml	4 tbsp	3fl oz
100ml		4fl oz
150ml	¼ pt	5fl oz
290ml	½ pt	10fl oz
290ml	½ pt	10fl oz
575ml	1 pt	20fl oz
700ml	1 ¼ pt	25fl oz
850ml	1 ½ pt	30fl oz
1l	1 ¾ pt	35 fl oz